Take a trip to
KENYA

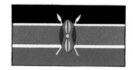

Keith Lye

General Editor
Henry Pluckrose

Franklin Watts

London   New York   Sydney   Toronto

Facts about Kenya

Area:
582,646 sq. km.
(224,961 sq. miles)

Population:
18,750,000

Capital:
Nairobi

Largest cities:
Nairobi (828,000)
Mombasa (342,000)
Kisumu (153,000)
Nakuru (93,000)

Officiallanguage:
Swahili

Religions:
Traditional religions,
Islam, Christianity

Main exports:
Petroleum products,
coffee, tea, cement, hides,
meat

Currency:
Kenya shilling

Franklin Watts Limited
12a Golden Square
London W1

ISBN: UK Edition 0 86313 270 7
ISBN: US Edition 0 531 10011 1
Library of Congress Catalog
Card No: 85–50163

© Franklin Watts Limited 1985

Typeset by Ace Filmsetting Ltd,
Frome, Somerset
Printed in Hong Kong

Maps: Tony Payne
Design: Edward Kinsey
Stamps: Stanley Gibbons Limited
Photographs: Zefa; Popperfoto, 7; Paul
Forrester, 8; Camerapix Hutchison, 11,
12, 14, 20, 21, 22, 24, 25, 31; Robert
Harding, 30; J. Allan Cash, 23; Bruce
Coleman Ltd, 13
Front cover: Zefa
Back cover: Camerapix Hutchison

Kenya is a country in East Africa. It is a little larger than France. Kenya is on the equator and low-lying areas are hot. But the southwest contains high, cool uplands and mountains. The snow-capped Mount Kenya is the highest peak, at 5,199 m (17,057 ft).

Kenya has beautiful national parks and reserves, which contain a great variety of animals. Here, tourists on safari enjoy a close-up view of an elephant in Amboseli National Park. Safari is a word in Swahili, the official language, for an expedition.

These gazelle are grazing on the savanna of central Kenya. Savanna is grassland, often with scattered trees. Savanna covers much of Kenya, a mostly dry country with few real forests. Less than a sixth of Kenya is sure to get 760 mm (15 in) of rain a year.

Nairobi, Kenya's capital, was founded in 1899 as headquarters of the British railway built to link the port of Mombasa to the southwest uplands of Kenya and, later, to Uganda. Kenya later became a British colony.

Kenya became independent in 1963. The picture shows prime minister Jomo Kenyatta, wearing a dark suit and a red and black hat, watching a parade. Kenya became a republic in 1964. When Kenyatta died in 1978, Daniel Arap Moi became the President.

The picture shows some stamps and money used in Kenya. The main unit of currency is the shilling, which contains 100 cents. The note shows a picture of President Daniel Arap Moi.

WORLD
MAP

Kenya

SUDAN

ETHIOPIA

Turkana
Plateau

Lake
Turkana

Chalbi
Desert

UGANDA

Marsabit
Reserve

KENYA

SOMALI
REPUBLIC

Mt Elgon

Kitale

L.Baringo

Samburu
Reserve

Eldoret

Kisumu

Nanyuki

Meru

Nakuru

Mt Kenya

Tana

Kericho

Nyeri

Lake Victoria

Masai
Mara
Reserve

L.Naivasha

Thika

Nairobi

Machakos

L.Magadi

Amboseli
Reserve

Tsavo
National
Park

Galana

INDIAN OCEAN

Mt Kilimanjaro

Mombasa

TANZANIA

A long deep rift valley runs
through Kenya from north to south.
This valley is 60 to 80 km (37–50
miles) wide. It was formed when a
block of land sank down between
long faults (cracks) in the Earth's
crust.

The rift valley floor is a dry region. But the valley contains several lakes. One of them, Lake Nakuru, is a bird sanctuary. It is the home of two million flamingoes and many other kinds of birds.

Lake Turkana is a long lake in the rift valley in northern Kenya. The Turkana people now live in this remote area. Around 1.75 to 2 million years ago, it was the home of various man-like and ape-like creatures, whose skulls have been found in the rocks.

Two Kenyans, Dr. Louis and Mary Leakey, dug up so many remains of man-like creatures in East Africa that many experts think that modern people probably evolved there. Here their son Richard and his colleague Kamoyo Kimeio have just found an interesting skull on the shores of Lake Turkana.

About 98 per cent of Kenya's
people are black Africans. They are
divided into about 40 groups. Each
has its own language and customs.
The Kikuyu, the largest group, live in
in the southwestern uplands. Most
are farmers.

Africa's largest lake, Victoria, is divided between Kenya, Uganda and Tanzania. Many of the fishermen around Lake Victoria belong to Kenya's second largest group, the Luo. Like the Kikuyu, most Luo are farmers.

The Masai are one of Kenya's
smaller groups. They are famous,
because many of them prefer the old
ways of life and reject western clothes
and ideas. The Masai, who were once
a warlike people, are also found in
Tanzania. Their main activity is
cattle raising.

Arab and Persian traders settled on the Kenyan coast from about AD 100. The Arabs introduced Islam, the Muslim religion, in the 7th century. This mosque (Muslim church) is on Lamu, an offshore island. A few Arabs still live in Kenya.

When Kenya became independent, many Britons became Kenyan citizens. Some own farms. Others work in various industries, including tourism. Here, the driver of a safari vehicle is feeding a wild monkey. He must be careful. Monkeys have sharp teeth.

Besides Africans, Arabs and
Europeans, Kenya also has citizens
of Indian and Pakistani origin. Many
of them are the descendants of people
who worked on the building of the
Kenya-Uganda railway. This Hindu
temple is in Mombasa, Kenya's
leading port.

Farming is the main activity in Kenya. It employs about four out of every five people. Coffee is the chief export crop. Much of it is grown on large plantations. Here, workers carry the coffee beans away from the fields. The beans are dried and then packed for export.

This picture shows workers picking tea, the second most valuable export crop. Nearly all of Kenya's farmland is in the southwestern highlands and near Lake Victoria. The north, far south and east are too dry for crops.

About half of the adults in Kenya cannot read or write. The government has recently supplied primary schools for nearly all children. Village schools like this one do not have the equipment that city schools have.

Religious groups run some schools. This child is studying the Koran, the Holy Book of Islam. Islam is important on the coast of Kenya. But 25 per cent of Kenyans are Christians and many more still follow local religions.

Many farmers work the land by hand. Their houses have thick thatched roofs and mud walls. Their main food is posho, or maize meal. When cooked, posho is eaten with beans and sometimes with meat or fish.

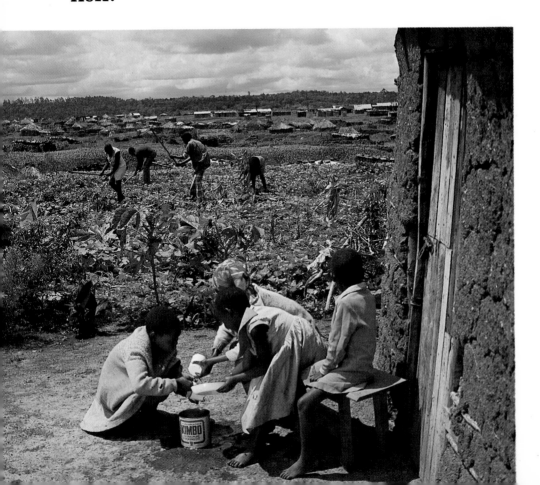

Kenyan women like bright clothes. This family lives in Lamu. The houses on the coast have thick walls that keep out the hot air during the day. This type of house was introduced into Kenya by Arab settlers.

Music and dance are enjoyed throughout Kenya. These dancers, wearing traditional dress, are Kikuyus. Traditional dances are one of the country's many tourist attractions. Tourism is increasing and more than 350,000 tourists arrive every year.

By world standards, Kenya is a poor country. City-dwellers, as here in Nairobi, are mostly better off than people in country areas. But Kenya's wealth has steadily increased since independence and it is now the most prosperous country in East Africa.

Index

Amboseli 4
Arabs 17
Asians 19

Brewery 25

Climate 3, 5
Coffee 20

Dancing 30

Education 26–27
Elephant 4

Farming 20–22
Flamingoes 11
Food 22

Gazelle 5

Hinduism 19
Houses 28–29

Industry 24–25
Islam 17, 27

Kamoyo, Kimeıo 13
Kenyatta, Jomo 7
Kikuyu 14

Lamu 17, 29
Languages 4, 14
Leakey, Richard 13
Luo 15

Maize 22, 28
Masai 16
Moi, Daniel Arap 7–8
Money 8
Monkeys 18
Mount Kenya 3

Nairobi 6, 31
Nakuru, Lake 11

Petroleum products 24
Prehistoric life 12–13

Railways 6, 19, 23
Rift valley 10–12

Savanna 5
Stamps 8

Tea 21
Tourism 4, 18, 30
Turkana, Lake 12–13

Victoria, Lake 15